GAME ON!

PAC-MAN

JESSICA RUSICK

Checkerboard Library

An Imprint of Abdo Publishing
abdobooks.com

abdobooks.com

Published by Abdo Publishing, a division of ABDO, PO Box 398166, Minneapolis, Minnesota 55439. Copyright © 2022 by Abdo Consulting Group, Inc. International copyrights reserved in all countries. No part of this book may be reproduced in any form without written permission from the publisher. Checkerboard Library™ is a trademark and logo of Abdo Publishing.

Printed in the United States of America, North Mankato, Minnesota
052021
092021

THIS BOOK CONTAINS
RECYCLED MATERIALS

Design: Aruna Rangarajan, Mighty Media, Inc.
Production: Mighty Media, Inc.
Editor: Rebecca Felix
Design Elements: Shutterstock Images
Cover Photographs: Fuad Suedan Diaz/Flickr; Gamerscore Blog/Flickr
Interior Photographs: ArcadeImages/Alamy, p. 21; Barry Brecheisen/AP Images, pp. 7, 28 (bottom left); Bryan Ochalla/Flickr, p. 15; Fuad Suedan Diaz/Flickr, p. 25; Gamerscore Blog/Flickr, p. 25 (top); Jason Newton/Flickr, p. 18; Manuel García Melgar/Flickr, p. 27; Manuel Sagra/Flickr, p. 9; Picasa/Flickr, pp. 13, 28 (top); pixy.org, pp. 23, 29; Rob Fahey/Flickr, p. 5; RV1864/Flickr, p. 19; Ryan Somma/Flickr, p. 24; Sergey Galyonkin/Wikimedia Commons, p. 17; Shutterstock Images, pp. 11, 28

Library of Congress Control Number: 2020949743

Publisher's Cataloging-in-Publication Data
Names: Rusick, Jessica, author.
Title: PAC-MAN / by Jessica Rusick
Description: Minneapolis, Minnesota : Abdo Publishing, 2022 | Series: Game On! | Includes online resources and index.
Identifiers: ISBN 9781532195808 (lib. bdg.) | ISBN 9781644945483 (pbk.) | ISBN 9781098216535 (ebook)
Subjects: LCSH: Video games--Juvenile literature. | Pac-Man (Game)--Juvenile literature. | Nintendo video games--Juvenile literature. | Maze puzzles--Juvenile literature. | Video games and children--Juvenile literature.
Classification: DDC 794.8--dc23

NOTE TO READERS

Video games that depict shooting or other violent acts should be subject to adult discretion and awareness that exposure to such acts may affect players' perceptions of violence in the real world.

CONTENTS

AN ICONIC GAME

A yellow circle moves through a maze, eating **pellets** in its path. PAC-MAN is on the move! Four colorful ghosts chase him as he eats. Just as a ghost is about to close in, PAC-MAN eats a glowing power pellet. The ghost turns blue and abandons its chase. The newly powerful PAC-MAN turns and eats the ghost! Then he eats the rest of the pellets. The level is cleared.

PAC-MAN is the most successful **arcade** game of all time. Its title character and gameplay **revolutionized** gaming. Since his 1980 **debut**, PAC-MAN has starred in numerous games for arcades, home **consoles**, and smartphones. *PAC-MAN* remains one of the most iconic **franchises** in video game history.

WAKA WAKA

Fans love the *PAC-MAN* sound effects. One is the "waka waka" noise PAC-MAN makes when eating. *PAC-MAN* creator Toru Iwatani demonstrated the sound he wanted to create by eating fruit and making gurgling noises!

In 2016, *Guinness World Records* named PAC-MAN the "Longest Running Dedicated Video Game Character" in history.

PUCK-MAN

PAC-MAN's designer, Toru Iwatani, was born in Tokyo, Japan, in 1955. In 1977, he began working for Japanese game manufacturer NAMCO. At the time, **arcades** were growing in popularity in Japan and the United States. NAMCO wanted to move beyond manufacturing arcade games to designing one.

NAMCO asked Iwatani to develop an arcade video game. Iwatani wanted his game to be different than usual games, which he felt were too violent. Popular games such as *Space Invaders* and *Asteroids* involved shooting aliens. At the time, arcades were also considered places where only boys hung out. Iwatani noticed few girls at arcades.

Iwatani wanted his game to attract a **diverse** arcade crowd. His idea was to make a nonviolent video game with cute, fun **graphics**. He decided to base the game around eating. He felt the universal activity of eating would appeal to many types of people.

Toru Iwatani said he and a NAMCO team wanted *Puck-Man* players to feel like being chased was fun and not torture. So, they made sure the game's maze always had an escape route.

7

One day, Iwatani was eating pizza while sketching game designs. He realized a pizza that's missing one slice looks like a head with an open mouth. This inspired the shape of his game's main character. Iwatani was also inspired by a rounded version of the Japanese word character *kuchi*, which means "mouth."

In Japanese, *paku paku taberu* is a phrase for gobbling something up. Iwatani used this phrase to name the main character in his game. The character's name was first Pakkuman, and then PUCK-MAN.

Iwatani continued developing the game with nine other NAMCO employees. *PUCK-MAN* players moved the main character through mazes filled with **pellets**. Players had to eat the pellets and avoid being killed by ghosts.

Players could also eat a power-up called a power pellet. This allowed them to eat ghosts and temporarily defeat them. Iwatani's game was the first to feature power-ups, which give characters new or boosted powers.

PINBALL PASSION

Iwatani wanted to work on pinball machines when he started at NAMCO.

In May 1980, players tried out the game at an **arcade** in Tokyo. Their response was positive. It was time to test whether Iwatani's game would be a hit with players everywhere.

PAC-MAN MANIA

NAMCO released *PUCK-MAN* throughout Japan in July 1980. It was a hit! Within a year and a half, the company had sold 350,000 *PUCK-MAN* **arcade** cabinets. In October 1980, the game made its US **debut**. Its name had changed to *PAC-MAN*. But the game was the same. By 1982, US *PAC-MAN* games were collectively making $8 million each week.

PAC-MAN's success was due in large part to PAC-MAN himself. In other video games, players controlled **inanimate** objects. *PAC-MAN* was the first game in history that let gamers control a character. This **revolutionized** video games. In coming years, other companies released video games with characters players could control.

Fans couldn't get enough of *PAC-MAN*. From 1982 to 1983, a PAC-MAN cartoon aired on TV. And PAC-MAN was featured on products such as clothes, lunch boxes, and posters.

PAC-MAN's gameplay brought more people to arcades. Other games required moving a joystick while also pressing buttons. PAC-MAN only required a joystick.

MS. PAC-MAN

As *PAC-MAN* mania swept the nation, some companies began making games similar to *PAC-MAN*. One was the US gaming company General Computer Corporation (GCC). In early 1981, GCC made a game called *Crazy Otto*. *Crazy Otto* had multiple types of mazes, while *PAC-MAN* had only one.

In October 1981, GCC showed *Crazy Otto* to Bally Midway, the company that sold *PAC-MAN* games in the United States. Bally Midway thought *Crazy Otto* could be the **sequel** to *PAC-MAN*. GCC worked with Bally Midway to turn *Crazy Otto* into a *PAC-MAN* sequel called *Ms. PAC-MAN*.

Ms. PAC-MAN was released in the United States in February 1982. Players loved it! The game became the best-selling **arcade** game in the United States. *PAC-MAN* was second.

NAMCO knew about *Ms. PAC-MAN*. But the company did not play a large role in its creation. Instead, NAMCO released its own *PAC-MAN* sequel, *Super PAC-MAN*, later that year.

The game was much different from the original. Instead of eating **pellets**, PAC-MAN ate keys that opened doors to food and power-ups. Fans disliked these changes. So, *Super PAC-MAN* was not as successful as *PAC-MAN* or *Ms. PAC-MAN.*

ARCADE ADDITIONS

Bally Midway released several more *PAC-MAN* **arcade** games in the early 1980s. These included *Jr. PAC-MAN*, *Baby PAC-MAN*, and *Professor PAC-MAN*. These games introduced new elements. However, none were as successful as *Ms. PAC-MAN*.

NAMCO also released new *PAC-MAN* games. *PAC & PAL* came out in Japan in 1983. But *PAC & PAL* was not popular with fans. So, NAMCO decided to reinvent PAC-MAN in its next game.

NAMCO released *PAC-LAND* in 1984. The game was a **platformer** and **side-scroller**. Instead of moving through a fixed maze, players traveled left to right through colorful cartoon settings. They jumped to climb platforms and dodge obstacles.

Critics liked *PAC-LAND*. It also inspired other games.

PAC-MAN PALOOZA

Jr. PAC-MAN had larger mazes than *PAC-MAN*. *Baby PAC-MAN* was both a maze game and a pinball machine! *Professor PAC-MAN* was a quiz game. Players answered questions and solved puzzles.

① ゲーム内容

バックランドに迷い込んだ妖精をフェアリーの国に送り届けるのが今回のパックマンの使命。邪魔なモンスターたちをかわし、フェアリーの国へ行き、家族の待つ家に帰ってきてください。このゲームには8種類のトリップがあって、各トリップはそれぞれ4つのラウンドに分されています。最初の3ラウンドは妖精をフェアリーの国へ送る、4ラウンドめはパックマンの への帰り道です。では冒険の前にバックランドの不思な世界をご紹介しましょう。

街
かわいい街並。でもよく見ると窓や車にもモンスターが…。

砂漠
砂の上に不気味なドクロ。うっかり近づくと砂地獄に引き込まれるぞ。

森
木立や茂みからいきなり飛びだすホッパーに気をつけて。

モンスター屋敷
モンスターでいっぱい。行き止まりの扉はどうすれば開くかな？

橋
あちこち崩れた橋を飛び移突然吹き上水柱にご用心

山
崖の上や雲にて渡ろう。飛行に要注意

A Japanese *PAC-LAND* instruction manual. To complete each stage in the game, players had to return a lost fairy to its home in Fairyland.

Nintendo's *Super Mario Bros.* was influenced by *PAC-LAND*'s **side-scrolling** action.

NAMCO returned to the maze genre with 1987's *PAC-MANIA*. In another series first, this game was in **3D**! Critics gave the game positive reviews. But the *PAC-MAN* craze was fading.

FROM ARCADES TO CONSOLES

By the early 1990s, the *PAC-MAN* craze had died down. *PAC-MAN* began to slowly disappear from **arcades**. However, new *PAC-MAN* games would soon **debut** on home **consoles**.

PAC-MAN's at-home debut had been in 1982, on the Atari 2600. The game was based on the arcade version of *PAC-MAN*. However, its **graphics** and gameplay were very different. Many fans had been disappointed by the game. But *PAC-MAN* still became the best-selling Atari 2600 game of all time.

In 1993, NAMCO released *PAC-Attack* on the Sega Genesis and the Super Nintendo Entertainment System (SNES). *PAC-Attack* was a puzzle game. Instead of traveling through mazes, players stacked blocks.

PAC-In-Time debuted for the SNES and Nintendo Game Boy in 1995. Critics felt the **side-scroller** was

NEW THEMES

In *PAC-In-Time*, players traveled through different themed levels, such as a castle level or forest level.

PAC-MAN for Atari sold more than 7 million copies.

a creative new entry in the *PAC-MAN* series. Fans were excited to see where the **franchise** would go next.

PROGRAMMING GHOSTS

PAC-MAN's ghosts are an important part of the *PAC-MAN* **franchise**. Iwatani worked with *PAC-MAN*'s **programmers** to develop an **algorithm** for the ghosts' movements. This algorithm determined how the ghosts moved around the maze and interacted with PAC-MAN. Not all the ghosts chased behind PAC-MAN. Iwatani thought the game would be more fun if each ghost moved in its own pattern.

The red ghost, Blinky, chases PAC-MAN from behind. The pink ghost, Pinky, tries to get in front of PAC-MAN. The orange ghost, Clyde, either chases PAC-MAN or wanders off on its own. The **cyan** ghost, Inky, has the greatest range. Its behavior can **mimic** any of the other three ghosts!

NUMEROUS NAMES

The *PAC-MAN* ghosts' Japanese names translate to Chaser, Ambusher, Fickle, and Stupid. In the United States, these names were changed to Shadow, Speedy, Bashful, and Pokey. However, the ghosts are better known by their nicknames Blinky, Pinky, Inky, and Clyde.

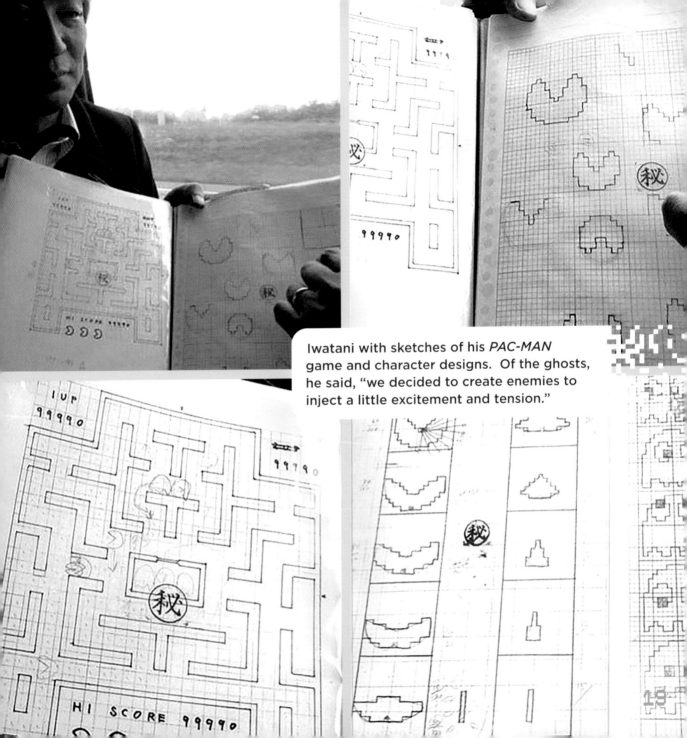

Iwatani with sketches of his *PAC-MAN* game and character designs. Of the ghosts, he said, "we decided to create enemies to inject a little excitement and tension."

PAC-MAN WORLD

In 1999, *PAC-MAN* neared its twentieth anniversary. That year, NAMCO released *PAC-MAN World* for the Sony PlayStation **console**. The game was the **franchise's** first **3D platformer**!

In *PAC-MAN World*, players still ate **pellets** and used power-ups to defeat ghosts. But the game also introduced new moves. Players could now bounce on top of enemies to defeat them. PAC-MAN could also roll backward up hills.

Critics praised the gameplay as fun and creative. The game had two **sequels**. *PAC-MAN World 2* was released in 2002. *PAC-MAN World 3* **debuted** in 2005. Each game featured a new story and new world for players to explore.

PERFECT SCORE

In 1999, American gamer Billy Mitchell was the first person to earn a perfect score of 3,333,360 points in *PAC-MAN*. Iwatani never imagined someone would reach the end of the game. So, there was no celebratory ending. Instead, the game displayed a **glitch!**

LAP 1/5

7TH

In 2006, NAMCO released *PAC-MAN World Rally*. It is a racing game version of *PAC-MAN World*.

21

NEW PLATFORMS

New *PAC-MAN* games were released into the 2000s. In 2005, *PAC-N-ROLL* **debuted** on the handheld Nintendo DS **console**. Users could roll PAC-MAN through **3D** levels using the console's touch screen.

In 2009, NAMCO released *PAC-MAN Remix*, made just for mobile phones. Users swiped to guide PAC-MAN through mazes. The game received positive reviews.

In 2013, *PAC-MAN and the Ghostly Adventures* aired on TV. Two new 3D **platformer** games based on it came out in 2013 and 2014. *PAC-MAN and the Ghostly Adventures* aired until 2015. That year, *PAC-MAN* also entered into the World Video Game Hall of Fame!

PAC-MAN ON GOOGLE

In 2010, Google released a playable *PAC-MAN* Google Doodle. Viewers could play a mini version of *PAC-MAN* on Google's homepage. The *PAC-MAN* Google Doodle was very popular. In just one day, users spent an estimated collective 4.8 million hours playing the game!

In *PAC-MAN and the Ghostly Adventures*, a teenage PAC-MAN and his friends guard their city from invading ghosts.

Meanwhile, new *PAC-MAN* mobile games were made. *PAC-MAN Bounce* was released in 2015. Instead of controlling PAC-MAN, users set up launch pads on a stage to control his movements. The mobile games *PAC-MAN Hats 1* and *2* followed in 2016 and 2017. In these maze games, users collected hats that gave PAC-MAN special abilities.

LEVEL UP!

Pac-Man Championship Edition DX

PAC-MAN Championship Edition DX was released by NAMCO in 2010. While similar to the original *PAC-MAN*, the game featured **updated** gameplay and new power-ups. Critics enjoyed its creative take on the original. By 2011, *PAC-MAN Championship Edition DX* had sold more than 200,000 copies.

The maze in each level of the original PAC-MAN gets more and more difficult as players advance.

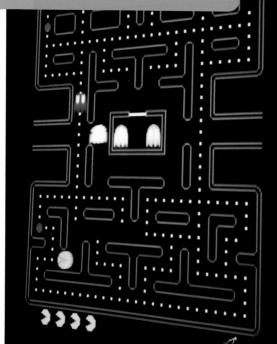

1980

PAC-MAN

+ Format: **Arcade** cabinet

+ Maze:
  - One maze layout across multiple levels
  - Each maze has 240 **pellets**

+ Gameplay:
  - Eat all the pellets to clear a level.
  - Four ghosts chase PAC-MAN.
  - Ghosts move faster as PAC-MAN levels up.

+ Power-Ups and Bonuses:
  - Power Pellets to eat ghosts
  - Bonus items (usually fruit) to gain extra points

2010

PAC-MAN CHAMPIONSHIP EDITION DX

+ Format: **Console** game for Microsoft's Xbox 360 and for the PlayStation 3

+ Maze:

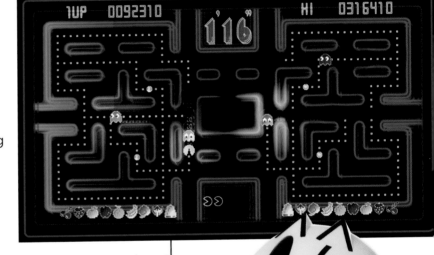

  - Maze divided into two sides
  - Maze shape changes as time progresses
  - Once one side of the maze is cleared, eating a bonus item causes **pellets** to refill on the cleared side.

+ Gameplay:

  - Score as many points as possible in timed rounds by eating pellets, fruit, and ghosts.
  - In addition to original four ghosts, "sleeping ghosts" awake to chase behind PAC-MAN when he passes by, forming a ghost chain.
  - Game speeds up as timer runs out

+ Power-Ups and Bonuses:

  - Power Pellets to eat ghosts
  - Bombs to send original four ghosts back to ghost pen at center of maze

PAC-MAN LEGACY

In 2020, *PAC-MAN* celebrated its fortieth anniversary. That May, gaming company Mojang Studios released a *PAC-MAN* **downloadable** content (DLC) pack for the video game *Minecraft* to honor the anniversary. With it, gamers could play a version of *PAC-MAN* within *Minecraft*!

Also in 2020, NAMCO partnered with Amazon Games to launch *PAC-MAN Live Studio*. This game would be built into the video game streaming platform Twitch. In the game, users could play the original *PAC-MAN* or new mazes. Players could also build their own mazes.

NAMCO also released the *PAC-MAN Geo* app in October 2020. Using Google Maps, players could turn maps of nearby streets into *PAC-MAN* mazes. PAC-MAN, ghosts, and **pellets** then appeared on the maps.

PAC-MAN was video gaming's first mascot to appear as a toy and on books, clothing, and board games. Forty years later, PAC-MAN is still an icon!

PAC-MAN remains one of the most recognizable video game characters in the world. For decades, players have enjoyed *PAC-MAN* across different platforms and **consoles**. And the yellow **pellet**-chomper is still hungry for more!

TIMELINE

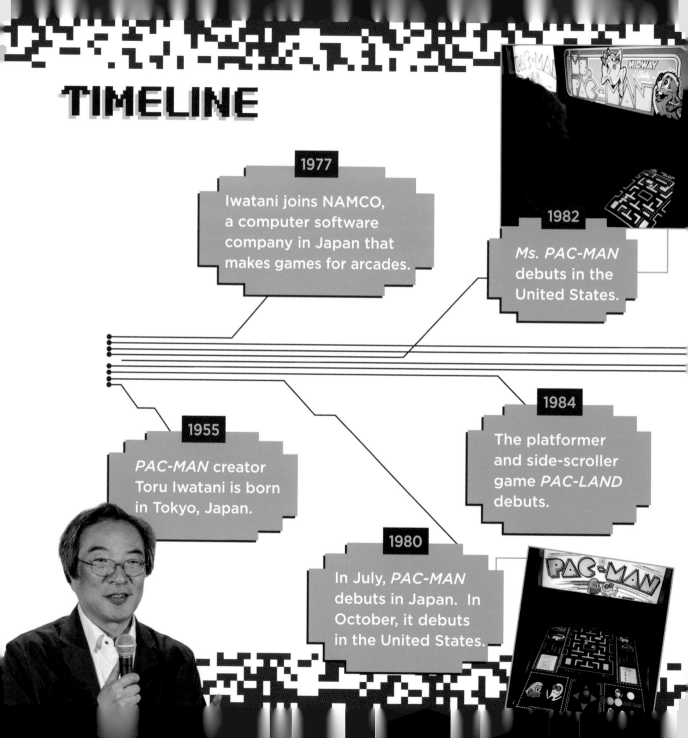

1977

Iwatani joins NAMCO, a computer software company in Japan that makes games for arcades.

1982

Ms. PAC-MAN debuts in the United States.

1955

PAC-MAN creator Toru Iwatani is born in Tokyo, Japan.

1984

The platformer and side-scroller game *PAC-LAND* debuts.

1980

In July, *PAC-MAN* debuts in Japan. In October, it debuts in the United States.

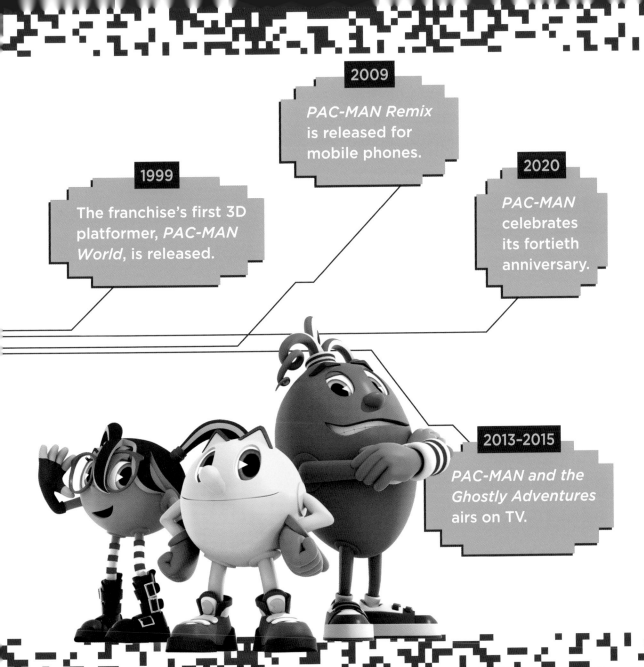

1999

The franchise's first 3D platformer, *PAC-MAN World*, is released.

2009

PAC-MAN Remix is released for mobile phones.

2020

PAC-MAN celebrates its fortieth anniversary.

2013–2015

PAC-MAN and the Ghostly Adventures airs on TV.

GLOSSARY

algorithm—a set of steps that are followed in order to solve a mathematical problem or to complete a computer process.

arcade—a business in which electronic game machines, such as pinball, can be played for entertainment.

console—an electronic system used to play video games.

cyan—a greenish-blue color.

debut (DAY-byoo)—to first appear. A first appearance is a debut.

diverse—made up of people who are different from one another.

downloadable—able to be transferred from a computer network to a single computer or device.

franchise—a series of related works, such as movies or video games, that feature the same characters.

glitch—a minor malfunction.

graphics—images on the screen of a computer, TV, or other device.

inanimate—not living.

mimic—to imitate or copy.

pellet—a small, rounded mass of substance.

platformer—a video game in which the player-controlled character moves and jumps across platforms of varying heights while avoiding obstacles.

programmer—a person who writes computer software.

revolutionize—to change fundamentally or completely.

sequel—a movie, game, or other work that continues the story of a previous work.

side-scroller—a video game in which the action is viewed from the side as the player-controlled character moves across the screen, usually from left to right.

3D—having length, width, and depth, or appearing to have these dimensions. *3D* stands for "three-dimensional."

update—to make something more modern or up-to-date.

ONLINE RESOURCES

Booklinks
NONFICTION NETWORK
FREE! ONLINE NONFICTION RESOURCES

To learn more about *PAC-MAN*, please visit **abdobooklinks.com** or scan this QR code. These links are routinely monitored and updated to provide the most current information available.

INDEX